THE
IRIS

THE IRIS

the rainbow flower

Photographs by Josh Westrich

Texts by Ben R. Hager

With 146 illustrations,
73 in colour

THAMES AND HUDSON

Josh Westrich is particularly grateful to Helene von Stein-Zeppelin,
Laufen, West Germany, and Piet van Veen, Vira-Gambarogno, Switzerland,
for their advice and support.

Art Direction: Rüther & Rüther

Phototypeset by Keyspools Ltd, Golborne, Lancs
Printed and bound in Japan by Dai Nippon

CONTENTS

Introduction

THIS BOOK has primarily been produced to present the beautiful and artistic floral portraits of the iris by the German photographer Josh Westrich. For most of us the photographs would be enough. For others a few words about the pictures add interest. The photographer has captured the essence of one of the most popular types of iris – the tall bearded – but the history of the flower itself goes back almost to the beginning of our civilization.

Perhaps you did not know that there are many different types of iris being grown in gardens around the world. Many people are not aware that the iris is second only to the rose in popularity with gardeners everywhere. It is the most highly favoured flower by amateur hobbyists who create new cultivars for growing in the garden. Most of the hybridizing or breeding for new varieties of roses is undertaken by professionals in big commercial firms. At least half of the breeding of irises, on the other hand, is done in backyard gardens and, although some of these breeders may also be commercial growers and sellers of irises in a small way, their interest is not in getting rich but in pursuing their hobby.

There are over thirteen national iris societies in the world today, each devoted to furthering knowledge of this beautiful flower. The American Iris Society (AIS), founded in 1920, was probably the first society to be organized around the single interest of the genus *Iris*. The AIS has the honour of being the international registry for named cultivars of iris. Indeed, such is the interest in the iris that there are now six volumes of registrations; they give the name of the cultivar and its description, the parentage of the cultivar, specific botanical information, the name of the breeder and the dates of registration and introduction to the market. Many of the registrations can be traced all the way back from the cultivar in question to some of the wild species that were its ancestors, in some cases fifteen or twenty generations.

This book lays the emphasis on the photographs of the iris: by assimilating the intrinsic beauty of the flowers expressed in the photographs we can appreciate the iris the more – the words are intended to enhance the memories.

History

'Iris' – the name of the Greek goddess of the rainbow who loaned her name to a whole group of flowering plants. Her name was particularly appropriate for the flower with the wide range of rainbow colours – the iris itself.

The iris first appears some 3,500 years ago as a hieroglyph carved in stone during the reign of the Egyptian Thotmes III. It is illustrated with a listing of medicinal plants. Irises would have had to be imported into Egypt, though not from far away, for some of their natural habitats were to be found just north and east of Egypt in what is now Israel and Syria. Indeed, there are those historians who think that 'the lilies of the field' mentioned in the Bible were in fact irises. If that is the case, then the type of iris was probably the aril iris, *Iris oncocyclus*, native to the deserts of that area (described in fuller detail on page 28).

More spectacular is a life-size painting in full colour on the wall of the Palace of Knossos (on the island that is now Crete) which goes back to approximately 1,500 BC. It portrays a royal prince strolling through a field of waist-high irises. The irises are not identifiable, having been rendered in a highly stylized fashion (the painter was probably relying on a faulty memory, without a fresh flower to hand), but the foliage and seed pods lead us to suppose that the irises were the bulbous *Iris xiphium* which grew along the coast of North Africa. The maritime traders of the Minoan island may have seen these flowers, even if they did not actually bring them home. *Iris xiphium* does not grow to waist height, but it is quite likely that the artist felt obliged to exaggerate in a painting of royalty.

Many years later Theophrastus (c.371–287 BC), the early Greek philosopher and botanist, mentioned the iris in his work on the classification of plants. He gathered a great deal of information in his thesis which has, amazingly, come down to us intact. It is available in book form in an English translation with the title *Inquiry Into Plants*. Theophrastus didn't actually use the word 'iris' to describe the flower, but his translator identified it as *Iris pallida*, the wild iris found predominantly in Yugoslavia today. At the time these irises grew in abundance in what was then known as Illyria (now Yugoslavia). To the Greeks the iris was important for its commercial value as a source of perfume. Theophrastus, therefore, was not concerned with the beauty of the iris flowers but with the 'rhizomes' or rootstock from which the distinctive scent could be obtained. He recounted how those workers who peeled the iris rhizomes before drying them were afflicted with sores and rashes of the hands. It is now known that iris rhizomes are mildly poisonous and do contain an alkaloid. However, this fact does not seem to bother gophers (from North and Central America) and voles (from Europe and North America) who voraciously consume large quantities with no apparent ill effects.

Several centuries after Theophrastus, another Greek writer, Dioscorides, compiled a compendium of plants for medicinal uses, which included a list of irises. The list, which appears in his *Vienna Codex*, strays from the main subject to mention the many colours of the iris and to include a drawing accurately representing the subject. Accompanying it were the suggestions that the iris plant could be used to remove freckles, stimulate tears, heal ulcers, rejuvenate the skin and induce sleep. Even gynaecologists of the time found uses for the extracts from iris plants. Finally Dioscorides came to the obvious conclusion, 'Irises are very useful generally.' And there the word 'iris' makes its appearance. But it is difficult to know whether the translator introduced a Greek word that he knew was associated with the plant or whether the name 'iris' was actually in use at that time.

The Greeks were obviously fond of the perfume of the iris rhizomes and may have carried them on long journeys or when they travelled to colonize distant shores. The distribution of the iris throughout the world known by the Greeks would indicate this fact. If we follow the routes taken by Alexander the Great's army into the eastern deserts and as far away as India, we find names, applied in the nineteenth and twentieth centuries, which correspond to places through which Alexander's army travelled many decades before Christ: *Iris mesopotamica*, *Iris kashmiriana*, 'Kharput'. If we list the names of other irises collected at the same time in Asia Minor, we have the names of places that the Greeks colonized on the Turkish shores: *Iris trojana*, *Iris cypriana*, *Iris junonia*, and the cultivars 'Amas' and 'Macrantha'.

These later collections were named after the locations in which they were found growing, but none of these places formed the natural habitat of these species. The small concentration of irises in these places makes it much more likely that they were distributed artificially – by man.

There has been a lot of controversy among botanists over the 'species' status of the tall bearded irises collected throughout Asia Minor and India. There are those who see this group of irises – those with the hairy, caterpillar-like beards – as originating from single or related clones of the same species which have been separated from their original habitat and, in isolation, have developed a few eccentric characteristics, though not enough to justify a classification distinct from the original species. A fuller explanation of the characteristics of the tall bearded iris is given on pages 15–16. The debate might seem to the layman to be of no consequence, yet this group of irises turned out to be the basis for the greatest revolution in the history of iris breeding. These irises were different from others collected elsewhere at the time. They were 'tetraploids', and they gave rise to the vast improvements in irises which we can appreciate today.

Development Processes

At this point, for those readers who are not of a biological bent, the terms 'diploid' and 'tetraploid' should be explained. The tetraploid species played an enormous role in the development of the irises we grow today and in those that are displayed for our pleasure in the photographs in this book. The following is an extreme simplification of the scientific processes involved, but it may help you to understand what happened when the forces of nature came together with human imagination.

All living organisms, animal and plant, are made up of cells. All of these cells share a similar basic structure and each contains a nucleus. Packed within that minute dot are many chromosomes, the exact number of which varies according to the particular organism. The chromosomes carry an arrangement of genes which direct the development and growth of the new organism after fertilization. The cells normally reproduce themselves exactly to create a whole structure. Only by the process of reduction division do they reduce the number of their chromosomes. In this procedure the chromosomes in the cell of one parent divide in half and recombine with the similarly divided chromosomes of the other parent, thus creating a new organism.

Because the genes on the chromosome can vary in each individual, the new combination of chromosomes carrying the selected genes from each parent brings about the differentiation of inheritance that is necessary to the process of evolution. The result is that no two individuals can be identical (the closest possibility would be identical twins but, even in that case, there are differences in development). The individual will retain the basic nature of the organism from which it sprang, be it cat, human or iris, but no two cats, humans or irises will be exactly the same. In the case of the iris, which is increased by division of the plant, each part will carry the same genes as every other and cannot vary except through mutation (a rare event) or seed.

Nature prefers the simplest way of doing things. The two-cell (diploid) building block is the simplest way to reproduce and grow, so most organisms are diploid, or were originally. But accidents happen, and if in fertilization the chromosomes do not divide properly and are inherited as a whole (known as an unreduced egg or gamete) instead of as a division, the resulting progeny will have cells with four sets of chromosomes instead of two. These cells are called tetraploid; they have, as a result of the accident, twice as many of everything. This is no longer the 'simple' way of nature, but it does bow to the idea that 'bigger is better' which exerted so much influence over the first and subsequent iris breeders. Tetraploidy can, and does, persist in nature, but where it has not happened through natural processes, as is the case with the bearded irises, man has learned chemically to induce tetraploidy, as in the beardless irises.

But why is so much fuss made over tetraploidy? By increasing the number of chromosomes in a cell from two to four, the number of possible combinations of the genes soars into millions. Not only is the size and hardiness of the plant or flower increased (a direct effect of the larger cells), but the possibilities of new colour and pattern combinations are also multiplied beyond imagination. Many different variations are now possible, though it may take some time before all the possibilities are realized, even with the boost of artificial mixing. The danger is that the new gene-splicing techniques may take all the fun out of breeding and experimentation, especially if, as is possible, they replace the practice of pollen dabbing.

Classification

As we have seen, irises were originally valued for their medicinal properties. The next mention of irises in historical literature takes place after medieval times. In 1551, William Turner (*c*.1520–68), the English physician, botanist and dean of Wells, published the *New Herball* in London. In a section entitled 'Of flour Delyce or flour Deluce' he gives directions for the medical use of iris rhizomes. He refers to the iris as 'Xyris or Spourqwurti', so the name we use today was close to being adopted then. The 'flour Delyce' or 'flour Deluce' were probably misspellings of the French 'fleur-de-lis', the stylized iris emblem associated with French royalty.

Twenty-five years later in 1576, Carolus Clusius (1526–1609) the French botanist, published descriptions of several species of iris, giving them names which have helped in their identification. He was the first to write about irises specifically as flowering plants, recording the many forms and colours he had seen while travelling in Europe. He was also the first to give a description of the oncocyclus iris, *Iris susiana*, which was based not on plants growing in the native desert but on those brought from Constantinople to Austria.

There are further mentions of the iris in literature but most of the writers merely quote Clusius. It wasn't until 1753 that the Swedish botanist Linnaeus (1707–78) published his system of botanical taxonomy for the naming and description of species and plants. Linnaeus included approximately twenty-four iris species, although a few of the names have since been proved to be incorrect. Nevertheless, his system of classification survived, proving its adequacy for the job, and is still in use by botanists. Linnaeus never acknowledged Clusius, but it is evident that he used Clusius's work as the basis for many of his descriptions.

Linnaeus was responsible for some of the confusion that has arisen over the tall bearded irises. He chose to describe the *type* of this section of the genus *Iris* as *Iris germanica*, probably because the plant was sent to him from a German garden.

In fact, *Iris × germanica* is a natural hybrid, not a species at all, and it does not grow wild in Germany. So the tall bearded iris has been saddled with the epithet 'German iris' over the years, even though the title is completely inappropriate and is now no longer permitted.

The hybrid nature of *I. × germanica* was not disclosed until the 1920s, when it was proven through chromosome counting. W. R. Dykes, however, was aware of its hybridity as early as 1913, before chromosomes were even recognized. He notes the fact in *The Genus Iris* of 1913, one of the great events in the history of the iris. Two men were directly responsible for the knowledge collected in this monumental work.

Sir Michael Foster (1836–1907) was the first individual seriously to set about collecting and growing the actual iris species from the wild. He had connections with wild plant collectors, friends and missionaries throughout the world, and was thus able to gather a notable garden full of iris species at his home in Shelford, England. He kept careful records and detailed drawings of the plants as they grew. He separated out and described many of the wild irises that were obviously different, gave them specific names and published the names and descriptions in the botanical magazine, the *Gardener's Chronicle*.

Foster cross-pollinated many of these irises. He was the first to grow arilbred seedlings and the Spuria 'Monspur' which made such an important contribution to the colour of Spuria irises (see pages 36–37). But, most importantly, he was the first in England to receive and grow the large irises from collectors in Asia Minor. These later became known as the tetraploid species that led to the great improvements in irises.

Foster died in 1907 but he left many hybrids of these new and larger irises which were introduced by Robert Wallace, a nurseryman of the period. Among these were some that appear in the complete family trees of many iris cultivars today: 'Caterina', 'Crusader', 'Kashmir White', and 'Lady Foster'.

It was Sir Michael Foster who encouraged another interested friend, William Rickatson Dykes (1877–1925), to continue the study of the whole genus and report on it, a task that Foster himself refused to undertake. Dykes did this job very thoroughly. He published two other books after his masterpiece *The Genus*

Iris (1913): *A Handbook of Garden Irises* (1924), and *Irises* (1930). It was his belief that a botanist should glean as much knowledge of the iris species as possible by taking notes in the wild, studying irises in the herbaria of Europe and America and actually growing them before writing anything about them. Dykes's garden grew from the donations of Foster and was increased by seeds and plants of wild irises sent from all over the world. All the drawings of the species irises in *The Genus Iris* were made in his garden by C. W. Johnson with the exception of *Iris lortetii* which was drawn from a growing plant in a garden in the south of France.

Considering the large amount of work that went into the monograph, it is understandable how *The Genus Iris* is still used today as the system on which taxonomy is based. Much new and corrected material has been added to the knowledge of irises since 1913, but *The Genus Iris* is the rock on which it is founded.

Botanists have for many years given names to plants and organized them into families, genera, and species. The categories are based on the morphology of the plants and divided into groups with certain similarities. Thus a species is a group of plants whose similarities unify them. They differ from other apparently similar plants, which nevertheless have some notably different morphological traits. Until recently divisions were based on purely visible features or a combination of traits such as seed shape, seed pod construction, or perianth tube measurements. The perianth tube is a hollow, tube-like structure of varying length lying between the flower and the ovary. However, methods of identifying species are bound to be influenced by the new information available about chromosomes. Breeding records of proven crosses should certainly be able to tell more about the relationship of two plants than information on the length of the perianth tube.

The following is a modified reproduction of the system of classification of the genus *Iris* by G. H. M. Lawrence. Excluded are a great many irises that are rarely found in our gardens; mostly they appear only in their wild habitats.

This list includes only those irises discussed in this book from the larger sectional groups to the individual species (the last group before the individual cultivar).

1 FAMILY: Iridaceae. There are many genera in this family, including the crocus, freesia and gladiolus.

2 GENUS: *Iris*. This is the only one of the genera in which we are interested. It contains *all* irises. The genus *Iris* is divided into subgenera and subsections:

a) Subsection Bearded Iris (Eupogon) with the following series:

> Miniature dwarf
> Standard dwarf
> Intermediate
> Miniature tall
> Border
> Tall

b) Subsection Hexapogon (Regelia)
   Subsection Oncocyclus (Onco) } — THE ARILS

c) Subsection Beardless Iris (Apogon)

> Series Sibericae 1 Subseries Sibericae, 2 Subseries Chrysographes.
> Series Californicae e.g. *Iris douglasiana, Iris innominata, Iris tenax* and others.
> Series Spuriae e.g. *Iris ochroleuca, Iris xanthospuria* and others.
> Series Laevigatae e.g. *Iris ensata (kaempferi), Iris laevigata, Iris pseudacorus, Iris versicolor, Iris virginica*.
> Series Hexagonae e.g. *Iris giganticaerulea, Iris brevicaulis, Iris fulva, Iris nelsonii*, and, possibly, *Iris hexagona*.
> Series Tripetalae e.g. *Iris setosa, Iris tridentata*.

d) Subsection Evansiae e.g. *Iris gracilipes, Iris cristata, Iris lacustris, Iris japonica, Iris confusa, Iris wattii, Iris milesii, Iris tectorum*.

e) Subgenus Xiphium — THE BULBOUS IRISES

Irises are divided into two groups which resemble each other but which are only distantly related. Indeed, they cannot be interbred. These two divisions are the bearded irises with the hairy, caterpillar-like beards that seem to crawl out of the throat of the flower, and the beardless irises which do *not* have these beards. A very definite distinction, you must agree. However, the beardless irises often have a yellow, lance-shaped mark, which lies in the same position as the beards of the bearded irises. One further, but less visible, division is made among beardless irises. Some are bulbous irises with onion-like storage units. Others, non-bulbous irises, have as their rootstock a rhizome, that is a solid, horizontal stem with roots along one side.

In the classification of plants, the genus *Iris* is a large family of plants with distinct characteristics. An iris is a flower with various parts that come in sets of three: three upright standards (most of the time), three flaring to downhanging falls (nearly always), three styles with three stigmas, along which lie three pollen-bearing anthers, and a three-chambered seed capsule. In between the flower and the ovary lies the perianth tube which separates the iris from most of the other flowering plants in the Iridaceae family.

No other flowering plant can present us with the same magnificence of display as the iris yet exhibit such unqualified appeal in the individual flower. The architecture of the iris flower in all its forms is unique; every part is beautifully structured but is there for a purpose. As striking as the form may appear, it is in every detail a practical construction. The drawing on page 142 shows the different parts of the iris flower. The standards (up-curving petals) form an expansive and airy dome over the delicate sexual organs of the flower, not out of modesty but for protection from rain and the sun's heat. The falls (the lower petals) are the landing platforms for the insects which pollinate the flowers. The colourful patterns of the falls are designed to attract insects such as bees, while the bushy beards lead into the tunnel formed by the claw of the fall underneath and the arching style arm above and so to the sought-after nectar. There is, of course, a purpose in this tunnel: on the underside of the style arm is the pollen-bearing anther, placed so that the pollen is brushed off on the bee's back on its descent into the tunnel. At the outer end of the style arm is a petaloid projection, known as the style crest, which protects the lip at the end of the style arm. This stigmatic lip is devised to scrape off the visiting bee's back the pollen which it has gathered from another flower. In this ingenious way pollination of the flower takes place. However, this method is not suitable for the tetraploid species or the big hybrids found in our gardens today. The process probably developed using the honey bee to transport the pollen, but with the larger flowers, the new tetraploids, the honey bee is no longer big enough to make the clever mechanics work. Nowadays bumble bees are needed, though there are not enough of them to do the job. Very few open pollinated seed pods are found in a patch of tall bearded irises. Honey bees do collect pollen as well as nectar, as any iris breeder who lives near an apiary can testify, and they may accidentally pollinate a stigma from time to time, but they are not able to fertilize every type of iris as nature intended. Nature knew best; before man's experiments introduced the new tetrapoloids, pollination of the smaller diploids could be carried out without the intervention of man.

If all our gardens were allowed to run wild, it is unlikely that the tall bearded irises would survive for long. The plant would be able to adjust to natural weather and fertility conditions, but there would not be enough seeds to maintain a wild population.

In contradiction to that theory, *I. × germanica* has survived and spread (although some of its population has probably arisen from polyphyletic origins) with few if any seedlings being produced. No identifiable hybrids of *I. × germanica* have been reported from the wild. Two *I. × germanica* cultivars, *Iris albicans* and *Iris florentina*, have been distributed throughout the world by man: *Iris florentina* has been used as a source of perfume and *Iris albicans* as a plant for graves. *Iris albicans* was even found growing in the mountains of northern Mexico quite recently.

Another speciality of the iris plant is the strong, uprising stem with, ideally, three or four wide branches. Multiple buds open one after the other to reveal flowers of individual beauty. The branches place the flowers at various heights and so a satisfactorily rounded picture of the whole form is created. These big flowers create enough of a colourful effect on their own; they do not need to be crowded together to attract insects or gardeners.

The tetraploid tall bearded irises cover the whole colour spectrum, except that there is no true green or red, only dark, slightly brown reds and reddish crimsons. Other colours include near black, violet and purple, sky blue, true brown, orange, yellow, white, cream, and true pink. The reddish tones in the iris are not even part of the colour pink, as might be expected. This pink colour is somehow chemically associated with the yellow pigment in irises. There are also peach tones, salmon, apricot – all colours that are connected with pink and yellow and with the so-called tangerine beards, though the colour is more of a reddish vermilion. The iris also combines these colours in interesting patterns, such as 'plicata' – a stitched effect of a darker colour over a lighter background, usually brown over yellow or blue over white – or 'amoena', in which the iris has white standards with coloured falls.

Distribution of Bearded Irises

The natural habitat of the bearded iris species which are of horticultural importance begins in Portugal, continues across southern France, Italy, Yugoslavia, Greece, Austria, Hungary and down through the Balkan Mountains, across the north side of the Black Sea to the other large body of water, the Caspian Sea, and up to the Ural Mountains. Aril irises are native to the area east of the Caspian Sea and to Turkey, Syria, Israel, Iraq and Iran. The most dominant group of bearded irises to be found from Portugal to the Urals is the dwarf bearded iris, which ranges in height between 4 and 15 inches and has small plants and flowers. The Greeks probably didn't consider it worth mentioning, as it only grew 4 or 5 inches above the soil, even though the countless blossoms of *Iris attica* must have created quite a show on the hills east of Athens in the spring. Even in those days man was interested in species of a larger size, such as *Iris pallida* which grew in vast fields throughout Illyria. It is possible that the Greeks also found irises with even larger rhizomes there.

It wasn't until the mid-twentieth century that two tetraploid tall bearded irises (*Iris croatica* and *Iris macedonica* – a temporary name) were discovered in Yugoslavia, and a further one (*Iris varbossiana*) in the Balkans. It is very likely that the Greeks knew about these larger rhizome irises and they may even have carried them throughout the known world of that time. The Greeks were probably responsible for transporting the diploid species *Iris pallida* too, though it preferred cooler climates. Tetraploids, however, were able to survive more easily in the arid regions to which they were taken.

Also growing in the Balkans from Hungary down to the Black Sea was another important diploid, *Iris variegata.* The home territory of this iris on its western front brought it into contact with *Iris pallida.* Many wild hybrids of the two species were mistakenly collected as species in the nineteenth century, as we shall see later.

Of all the various species growing in this southern to central European location only two, *Iris pallida* and *Iris variegata*, played an important role in later breeding developments. It was found that when these species and their diploid offspring were crossed with tetraploids, occasionally sturdier irises with larger flowers resulted which would perform well in a variety of conditions. *Iris variegata* is arguably the greatest source of the colour variations in the later hybrids. It was the only one to have a yellow colour base and reddish tones in the falls. These two colours blended with the violet/lavender tones of *Iris pallida* and the tetraploid species resulted, with the vast array of colours we see in today's gardens.

Breeding

Over four hundred years ago Carolus Clusius wrote the now-famous line, 'Long experience has taught me that irises grown from seed vary in a wonderful way.' But it was not until the early nineteenth century that anyone took him seriously. At that time nurserymen started to take an interest in growing irises from seeds gathered from bee-pollinated pods. Many gardens of the time contained the two major European diploid species – *Iris pallida* and *Iris variegata.* A few natural hybrids collected in the wild were also probably grown. As it was believed that the wild hybrids were different species, they were given names such as *I. sambucina, I. amoena, I. squalens, I. neglecta,* or *I. plicata.* Later, when it was discovered that these irises were in fact hybrids, the names were used to describe the prominent colour patterns.

A French nurseryman called de Bure was the first to name an iris cultivar and to distribute it commercially. He used a Latinization of his own name for this first hybrid of 1822, 'Buriensis'. He was responsible for the subsequent interest in, and development of, iris varieties.

De Bure's work exerted an influence twenty years later on M. Lemon, a French nurseryman, who published a list of a hundred or more named varieties chosen from his seedling patch. Among these were 'Jacquesiana' (named after the friend who had led him into growing irises) and 'Mme Chereau', a blue and white plicata still found in iris collections devoted to the history of irises. M. Lemon continued his work and in 1840 introduced a variegata (an iris with yellow standards and reddish falls) under the name 'Honorabile' which is still being grown in modern miniature tall bearded iris collections. 'Honorabile' is notable for having sported (an unusual feat in irises anyway) more times than any iris on record. These 'sports' include 'Sans Souci' (a paler variegata), 'Sherwin Wright' (a yellow self – the petals are all the same colour), 'Kaleidoscope', in which the fall colour 'breaks' to yellow, blue or white, and 'Joseph's Coat', which has various flowers of either variegata or amoena or mixtures of anything in between – a variety with a truly unstable gene.

But these new cultivars were still only developed from pollination by bees – crosses unaided by man's intervention, apart from the fact that the plants were grown in the same garden. It was only in the last decade of the nineteenth century that the results of hand crosses became available. Goos and Koenemann in Germany and at least two breeders in England, Amos Perry and George Ruthe, produced such beautiful new hybrids that it was widely accepted no further improvements in form and colour could be made. Interest in iris breeding therefore declined.

The First Revolution

Little did the iris growers and breeders at the turn of the century realize that irises brought from Asia Minor were already available in gardens in England and France and that these were to become the precursors of a revolution that is still taking place and gaining momentum. What were these radically different irises? They were, of course, the tetraploid species. But the growers of the time did not know why these irises were radically different, though they admired the large size of the flowers and plants. The idea that bigger is better is not confined to the present age, as we have noted before. Enthusiasm for these bigger irises dwindled when it was found that they had a very limited range of colours (various shades of purple and lavender) and that they did not grow well in the colder, less temperate weather conditions found in the gardens of England and the Midwest of the United States. The small irises with which the breeders had been working were superior in both of these features: they were hardy to the cold and the colours ranged from deep purple and reddish tones through white, yellow, amoena, bicolour, and pastel blends. Breeders therefore took the obvious step of crossing these smaller irises with the larger ones. Their first attempts met with little success. Very few seeds were obtained and those that were produced seedlings that were, on the whole, sterile. The new hybrids were larger, but they had no other notable features. A small number were good enough to grow as garden plants but they contributed little to the development of the iris.

After persevering, the breeders produced new hybrids with the desired results – fertility and improved form. At the time these breeders were not aware that their new irises were tetraploid hybrids, derived from crossing the original tetraploid species with the rare unreduced egg in the diploid parent. Usually the crossing of diploid and tetraploid parents results in a triploid (one chromosome from the diploid parent and two chromosomes from the tetraploid parent), which is nearly always sterile. However, there are exceptions to the general rule. In a very small number of cases, triploid (pod) and tetraploid (pollen) crosses produce a fertile tetraploid offspring. These fertile triploids, however, are less common than mutant tetraploids, which occur because of an unreduced gamete in the diploid parent.

The iris world was not aware of the full implications until the early 1920s. Mendel had recorded the hereditary action of genes years before but, having no microscope, he had no way of knowing the mechanics of the inheritance, and his work had been ignored for many years. The botanist Strassburger had observed chromosomes in plants as early as 1882, but no one paid much attention to his findings either. Not until the 1920s and 1930s, when chromosome counting had become possible, did the iris world know exactly why the new species and hybrids were 'bigger and better'. The French botanist Dr Marc Simonet published in 1928, 1932 and 1934 long lists of chromosome counts of not only the new tetraploids, but also of the diploids and the dwarf bearded and beardless irises. His work sparked off new interest amongst breeders in developing improved irises.

The early breeders of the tetraploid iris must be credited for their pioneering work. The irises they produced were the basis of the magnificent creations we can appreciate in this book and our gardens today. Their curiosity and drive led to the stunning variations in colour and form of today's irises.

Most of the new European varieties were developed between 1890 and 1915. The French firm of Vilmorin were responsible for introducing several of these new tetraploids, including the important 'Oriflamme' and 'Ambassadeur'. Sir Michael Foster undertook some valuable work in this field. Before his death he succeeded in developing several new tetraploid cultivars (see page 13). 'Lord of June' (Yeld), also introduced by Robert Wallace, was very successful at about this time. The most famous iris of this group, 'Dominion', produced from a cross with the tetraploid 'Amas', was raised by A. J. Bliss, a retired engineer, in England. It was widely used by other breeders who valued it for its texture and velvety finish.

American breeders also had a hand in the development of the iris: Grace Sturtevant (Massachusetts) used 'Caterina' for her 'Sherbert'. E. B. Williamson (Indiana) raised 'Lent A. Williamson', an offspring of 'Amas'. Among the early Californian breeders, William Mohr produced the pale-blue 'Conquistador' and the white 'Purissima' by crossing 'Caterina' × 'Kashmir White' with 'Conquistador'; while Sydney B. Mitchell, the Californian breeder, did invaluable work on the development of the yellow irises. The Sass brothers, Hans and Jacob, from Nebraska, raised some notable hybrids: 'Joysette', 'King Tut' and 'Rameses'.

Nearly every prominent breeder of that time succeeded in developing at least one great iris by crossing the tetraploid species with the older diploids; some had many such hybrids attributed to their name. All of these irises and the European originals were used extensively in gardens on both sides of the Atlantic, though they did not gain world-wide distribution until after the First World War.

The Pink Revolution

Tetraploidy was not only responsible for bringing irises of increased size into our gardens. It also introduced a whole range of new colours.

The colour pink did not make its appearance in irises until the tetraploid revolution. Cross-breeding with orchid pinks or red-toned irises had not resulted in the desired colour. Breeders of the time could not understand why their efforts met with so little success. Then, all of a sudden, pink appeared in several irises at about the same time, together with tangerine beards, the constant companion of pink-coloured petals.

All of these pinks came into existence within a period of approximately ten years. A colour that had never been seen before in irises was suddenly found in the gardens of breeders who had been working with irises of untraceable backgrounds. In those days breeders were not, on the whole, very concerned about keeping written records of crosses. Similar events have taken place in other histories of breeding, but never with the same speed or impact.

There was a good reason for the suddenness of the occurrence of pink irises. Pink is a recessive colour. In other words, all four chromosomes in the tetraploid hybrid have to carry from both parents a gene with the pink factor in order for pink seedlings to be produced. It was for this reason that the colour pink took so long to make its appearance. It could not be achieved in diploids which have only two cells.

'Goldfish' (Wareham 1925) was the first tangerine-bearded pink iris to be registered. It was an ugly little thing and was never used for breeding, but it did contain the four necessary genes, as later crosses to pink irises proved.

The first clear pink, in fact, was 'Sea Shell', which was raised about the same time as 'Goldfish', though it was not registered until much later. The breeder of 'Sea Shell', P. A. Loomis from Colorado, used this first true pink to raise further pink irises. In 1929 he registered 'Spindrift', the first popular pink iris, but he did not put it on the market until more than ten years later.

In 1934 Sydney B. Mitchell introduced his successful yellow 'Happy Days'. Apart from bringing yellow as a colour into the new tetraploid irises, 'Happy Days' was important for its connection with a sister seedling (a seed from the same pod) which was a pale pink with tangerine beards. Mitchell named the latter

'Isabelina', though he never registered it or introduced it commercially. It was, however, used extensively for breeding.

In Nebraska the Sass brothers' experiments led to 'Flora Zenor', the deepest pink of the group. 'Pink Cameo' (Orville Fay 1944), was the truest pink iris with the best shape. Another notable pink iris, 'Melitza' (1940), was raised by Elizabeth Nesmith, a commercial grower and iris breeder from New England. Though its colouring – a dull pinkish beige with tangerine beards – was unexceptional, it played an important role in breeding.

The appearance of the colour pink in several separate locations through the efforts of different breeders was a truly intriguing phenomenon. Most of the other prominent colours could be traced to irises in the background. Pink was a new colour. The limitation of colour tones to the shades of purple and violet in tetraploids meant that most of the colours in the new group of tall bearded irises had to come from the diploids. Plicatas, variegatas, blends, reddish tones and yellow definitely came through the diploids. The only source for the colour yellow was the species *I. variegata*, which, as the name implies, was a variegata with yellow standards and reddish falls. Yellow already existed in some diploids which had found their way into the tetraploid lines, but it required some original thinking to produce a good tetraploid yellow. Sydney B. Mitchell eventually succeeded by crossing some brownish irises with white ones. W. R. Dykes also produced a tetraploid yellow but the parentage is not known.

Not all of the work on pink colour took place in America. Sir Cedric Morris, the English amateur iris breeder, produced 'Edward Windsor' (1945), the offspring of two yellow plicatas. You can find a first-generation seedling of 'Edward Windsor' – 'Constant Wattez' (Piet van Veen 1959) – on page 54.

The colour pink, then, formed the second revolution in iris breeding history. It is the only completely new colour to be introduced through tetraploidy so far.

The Bicolour Revolution

The American breeder Paul Cook brought about the third iris revolution. When he crossed an iris he knew as *Iris reichenbachii* and a tall bearded iris, he was rewarded with a standard dwarf seedling which he named 'Progenitor'. It proved to have a dominant gene that suppressed colour in the standards. When it was crossed with irises of any colour, the resulting seedlings had white, cream, pale-blue, or yellow standards and deep-coloured falls of another shade. Since then, the new bicolour irises have flooded the market. Older types of bicolours, especially amoenas, were recessive and therefore difficult to reproduce as seedlings. Nowadays it is easy, almost too easy, to produce these beautiful new bicolours.

Other Bearded Irises

NOVELTY IRISES

Novelty irises are gaining popularity. The so-called 'Space Age' irises are particularly appreciated for their extra appendages which rise up from the ends of the beards and give them the air of communication satellites. Some of the extensions are like pointed horns and are sometimes bearded, others have long delicate filaments with decorative tips. Others display 'flounces' which look like horns at first but turn into ruffled petaloids. The unusual splashes of one colour over another (usually white), caused by an unstable gene determining colour, are found in irises as well as roses, camellias and other flowers and make a different and appealing pattern. The 'flat' irises are mutations that produce six falls but no standards. This mutation is also popular in Japanese, Siberian and Louisiana irises. Mutations in form or colour in the tall bearded irises have been reason enough in themselves for gardeners to grow them, mostly for fun, but the 'Space Age' iris group has been the only one susceptible to successful breeding and improvement programmes. The other novelty irises are rarer because no way has been found to establish the pattern in the seedlings which turn out to be monstrosities.

DWARF IRISES

The very smallest group of bearded irises, the miniature dwarf bearded (MDB) irises, are the first to flower. These tiny plants seem to share few of the characteristics of the giants which flower at the end of the season. The stems of the dwarfs range up to 8 inches while the flowers average 2 inches.

In the wild these dwarf bearded irises are more widely distributed than the rest of the bearded irises combined. The largest of these dwarfs, *Iris chamaeiris*, which comes in a limited colour range of yellow and violet, is found in Portugal, southern France and Italy. Further east, in Yugoslavia and Greece, lies the home of the dwarf irises *Iris pseudopumila* and *Iris attica*.

Iris pumila joins other dwarf species in the Balkan Mountains. It has been so successful as a species that it has migrated all the way from Yugoslavia through the Balkans and finally to the lower end of the Ural Mountains in central Russia, apparently without the aid of man. Indeed, it is the most widely distributed of the dwarf bearded irises. *Iris pumila* is the most important of the above species, both as a garden plant and as a breeder parent. It probably originated as a hybrid between two diploid species, *Iris attica* and *Iris pseudopumila*, and in the cross-breeding the chromosomes doubled, thus making *Iris pumila*, despite its small size, a tetraploid.

There are two other tetraploid species of dwarf irises growing in the Balkan Mountains: *Iris aphylla* and *Iris balkana*. They have the same number of chromosomes (forty-eight) as the tall bearded irises, unlike *Iris pumila* which has thirty-two. Although they are not spectacular or popular garden plants, both have made their mark in hybridizing with other, mostly larger, species. *Iris aphylla* has made notable contributions to the miniature tall bearded and the miniature dwarf bearded groups.

MEDIAN IRISES

No species, however, has made such an impression on so many different groups of bearded iris as *Iris pumila*. It is the dominant breeder parent in the miniature dwarf class; it is the virtual dictator in the standard dwarf bearded (SDB) series, the strain produced by the combination of *Iris pumila* and tall bearded irises. The cross, which dominates the median iris section (the group lying in size between miniature dwarfs and tall bearded irises), has been made many times and with many different parents from *Iris pumila* and the tall bearded irises and intercrosses between the usually very fertile progeny. This class has now swollen to include every colour and pattern available in either parental stock. These irises are highly valued for the large number of blooms, their varied colour and ability to bloom with and after the late daffodils. The plants make a neat low clump but are exceptionally vigorous and abundant in all but the most temperate areas.

Contrary to the earlier conclusions made concerning tall bearded irises, the standard dwarf bearded iris would probably succeed if left uncultivated in the wild. The flowers are easily pollinated and the seed germinates more abundantly and more quickly than other bearded irises. The plants are especially vigorous and tenacious, even under adverse conditions.

INTERMEDIATE BEARDED IRISES

The intermediate bearded irises, which range from 16 to 28 inches in size, arose from the cross of standard dwarfs (8 to 16 inches) and tall bearded irises (over 28 inches). They are intermediate not only in plant and flower size but also in season of bloom and make excellent garden subjects. They flower just after the standard dwarfs and just before the tall beardeds.

MINIATURE TALL BEARDED AND BORDER BEARDED IRISES

Two other median types, the miniature tall bearded and the border bearded, bloom at roughly the same time as the tall bearded varieties. The miniature tall bearded irises are scaled-down, miniature representations of their larger relatives. They have small, 3-inch flowers on branched, delicately constructed stems. These irises are the last stronghold of the diploid species, though tetraploidy is edging in to increase the range of colour and form. The tetraploids will probably not replace the diploids in this group, for the breeding potential is limited. It is hoped that the two types will be able to coexist, since both have different qualities to offer. The miniature talls and the next group, the border bearded irises, are limited to a height of between 16 and 28 inches. Border irises are half the size of tall bearded irises and are mostly small-flowered selections from tall bearded breeding. Efforts are being made towards breeding true border irises rather than waiting for them to appear by chance, and *Iris aphylla* is beginning to play a role in the hybridizing of this group. The plant and flower size of the miniature tall bearded and border bearded irises make them useful in a landscape setting. These two groups particularly appeal to those who are attracted to the diminutive forms of the usually larger iris plants.

Many of the bearded irises have made their home around the edges of the arid desert areas. The same conditions are favoured by some of the beardless irises to be considered later in this book. The aril group of bearded irises, found in the very arid regions of the Middle East, is divided into two sections, the oncocyclus and the regelia irises.

The 'oncos', to use their familiar name, are the fantasy irises. They are subtly coloured in mostly pastel shades; perhaps the desert sun was too fierce to allow the wide variety of colour found in other members of the iris family. Their exotic, sometimes extraordinary patterns consist of deeply etched, vertical veins, or heavy stitching in deep grey, maroon or near black. It is as though the plant were creating some protection for the succulent petal tissues from the relentless desert sun. Sometimes the pattern is so dense as to give a dark hue to the petals, often almost black, lying over a lighter tone. Even in the rare instances where the petal colour itself is dark, the overlying veining takes on near blackish tones. Even the diffuse beards are dark. On the upper to middle part of the fall is a concentration of dark, nearly always black, colour in the form of a solid round spot. This spot, the 'signal', is designed to attract insects. A few of the species will be coloured in warmer tones and the hybrids between onco species will sometimes vary greatly in the colour of the veining and signals; the latter have been noted in yellow or bright red instead of the usual blackish tones. The wide falls, in most cases, tuck under themselves, showing just enough surface to display the signal. The balloon-like standards are larger and form an extensive canopy over the centre of the flower. There is only one flower to each stem but each one lasts for several days, barring misfortune, in contrast to the three-day life of most other iris flowers.

The natural habitat of the oncocyclus iris ranges from Israel through Syria, Turkey, Iraq, and Iran. The other group of aril irises, the regelias, come from the arid regions east of the Caspian Sea. These irises grow very happily in the same dry conditions as the oncocyclus do. The main differences between the two groups lie in the chromosome count and the shape of the flowers. Instead of the bulging, bulbous flowers of the oncocyclus, the regelia is distinguished by its rather smaller flowers with narrower petals that are erect and hang down at the ends. Common characteristics of this group include veining, prominent colour and long beards. An exception is *Iris hoogiana* which has no marking, and is a silken lavender-blue colour.

Outside the Middle East, the aril group are strangers in a strange land. Being accustomed to very dry areas, they do not like being transplanted to so-called 'improved' conditions. They fare poorly in most gardens. Only fanatic gardeners should try to grow them and might be successful in giving them an artificial home.

There is, however, one consolation for those who are attracted to these eccentric members of the iris family. Because of the difficulty of growing aril irises out of their natural habitat, breeders tried to create new hybrids which retained many of the unusual patterns and striking colours of the species. Tall bearded irises were crossed with the aril irises and the result was 'the arilbreds'. Some difficulties were experienced in producing these new hybrids because of the varying chromosome counts in the irises: oncocyclus are twenty chromosome diploids, regelias are twenty-two chromosome diploids, whereas tall bearded irises are forty-eight chromosome tetraploids. However, breeders persevered and we now have a fertile race of arilbreds which combine the vigour of the tall bearded irises with the intriguing exoticism of the arils.

Though the arilbreds are easier to grow, they still need careful attention. They require good drainage to avoid soaking the rhizome, frequent division of the clumps (if the rhizomes are crowded rot is unavoidable), plenty of moisture during the spring, and then completely dry conditions from July to October, when watering may be started again in mild areas. Arilbreds should be transplanted often – as often as once a year, provided they are growing well and producing healthy plants – into alkaline soil (dolamitic limestone can be added to acid soils) with a fertilizer.

Culture of Bearded Irises

All other bearded irises are easy to grow, if the correct measures are taken. Good drainage is essential, especially in areas with summer rains. These irises should be planted on a hill or ridge with an irrigation ditch.

Plants perform well if they are transplanted every two to three years into soil which has not been used to grow irises for two or more years. It is a good idea to introduce a system which rotates other plants, flowering or vegetable, with the iris. This rotation method enriches the soil and should be used for all garden plants other than permanent perennials. Fumigation is the best way to renew the soil, but is not always convenient or possible.

These irises prefer neutral to lightly alkaline soils. A balanced fertilizer (one with 6% nitrogen, 9% phosphorus and 6% potash) should be added in the spring just before blooming, though these percentages vary according to the needs of the soil. Commercial fertilizers take six to eight weeks in the soil to affect the plant. Irises put on their most important and vigorous growth during the four to six weeks after blooming; it is at this time that fertilizer and moisture are most needed by the plant. For it is in this period that the new rhizomes and the flowering buds are being developed for the following year's growth and bloom and the fertilizer is now ready to be ingested by the roots. If manure is used, it should not come into contact with the plant. Finally, follow local recommendations for the treatment of insects and disease.

Future Developments

So many changes have taken place in the tall bearded iris group over the last one hundred years that it is difficult to imagine what further improvements could be made in the future. In my opinion, however, another revolution is imminent. One frequent complaint amongst gardeners is that irises bloom for too short a time. Some breeders have been working on this problem for years, almost since the first hand crosses were made. Their efforts have met with some success. Some irises do rebloom regularly in spring and later again in autumn but the flowers are rather poor in quality. A small group of enthusiastic breeders have continued to seek improvements in the reblooming tendency, a natural feature of the iris, though no great strides have been made. Perhaps this area may be the next revolution in the iris world.

Indeed, more and more seedlings with no apparent genetic background for reblooming and even some new cultivars are producing unexpected flowers in the autumn. This talent is even being passed on to their offspring in increasing numbers. Could it be that irises have decided that they would like a larger part on the garden stage? Let us hope so. Of course better care and attention, by way of improved feeding and irrigation, has to be given to plants in order to support the extra effort entailed in remontancy.

Perfume from Irises

Before we leave the discussion of bearded irises behind, perhaps we should look at one of the main commercial uses of the iris – as a source of perfume. As we have seen, this application played a large part in the early history of iris. Nowadays orrisroot, produced from dried iris rhizomes, is still harvested on a large scale in Italy. *Iris florentina* used to be grown commercially for this purpose but *Iris pallida* now seems to have taken its place. In fact the rhizomes of almost any tall bearded iris can be used to create an intriguingly fragrant powder. The rhizomes of the tall bearded iris 'Apropos' produce a particularly pleasant, intense violet odour which lasts for a long time.

To obtain the best results, it is necessary to break or cut open a rhizome and smell the freshly opened surface. If the scent is attractive, set aside some rhizomes of the cultivar for further treatment. The best time to undertake this task is at the moment of transplanting, when the rhizomes have to be separated. It is also worth keeping an eye open for soft rot in the rhizome. Most soft rot stinks offensively, but once in a while you will come across a completely enchanting fragrance. Rhizomes from such a clone can be used for orrisroot.

It is not difficult to produce orrisroot provided various steps are taken. Firstly, the rhizomes have to be dug up and peeled. For those with sensitive hands, rubber gloves should be worn. As far back as 350 BC Theophrastus warned that rhizomes could cause rashes. After the rhizomes have been sliced thinly, they should be dried in a warm, dark place for approximately one year. It is not a good idea to use a fuel-produced heat which ruins the final smell. Alternatively, the rhizomes may be hung out to dry in lines, a method followed by the early Greeks. When the sliced rhizomes have dried thoroughly, they should be ground to a powder. A food blender works very well for this task. Finally, the powder should be placed in covered dishes with a vent-hole or in cloth bags in a position where the scent can be enjoyed. The perfume will last for three to four years, depending on the rhizome used.

Beardless Irises

DISTRIBUTION

Beardless irises are much more widely distributed throughout the world than the bearded irises. In their many variations, beardless irises circumscribe the northern hemisphere. They are found from the Arctic (*Iris setosa*) to the Gulf of Mexico (*Iris hexagona*) and Hong Kong (*Iris speculatrix*). The wide separation of some of the related beardless species, such as the Siberians of Europe and Asia from the series Californicae, and the discontinuity of the specific habitats of the species in the subsection Evansiae, could lead to the conclusion that the ancestors of the current species were in existence prior to the continental shifts.

SERIES TRIPETALAE

Iris setosa, the most northerly iris, is the only species to be found on two separate continents: in Asia and in both Alaska and Labrador on the North American continent. This species is a very decorative plant but demands cold, wintry conditions, growing poorly, if at all, in areas south of the northern states in the USA. There is a triploid form, said to be collected in the wild in northern Japan by the late Emperor Hirohito, that enjoys more temperate climes, such as California. Known as *Iris setosa* 'Nasuensis', it is a vigorous and welcome addition to such garden locations. A close relative, and the only other species in this Tripetalae series, is a subtropical bog plant, *Iris tridentata*, found wild in swampy areas in the states of Georgia and the Carolinas. The two irises in this series are characterized by three falls and virtually no standards; what standards there are are reduced to mere projections.

SERIES LAEVIGATAE — the bog or water irises

Moving down from the Arctic along the eastern side of the North American continent, the next large population of irises is *Iris versicolor*. This iris is thought to be a hybrid between *Iris setosa* and the next species geographically, *Iris virginica*. *Iris versicolor* has the highest chromosome count of any iris species (108). It is an example of a hybrid population that doubled its chromosome count and developed enough differing characteristics to qualify for specification.

Iris versicolor and *Iris virginica*, like all of their close relatives (with the possible exception of *Iris setosa*) belong to the series Laevigatae which are bog or water irises. *Iris virginica* takes over from the geographical area of *Iris versicolor* in ponds and marshes and continues southward. Some plants from the *Iris virginica* species can compete in size with the giant Laevigata found in Europe. *Iris pseudacorus*, the only yellow-flowered member of this series, can grow to a height of 6 or 7 feet. A vigorous and prolific plant, it is found in stream beds and lake shores all over the world but is *native* only to Europe. *Iris laevigata* (or Kakasubata to the Japanese) is the oriental representative of the series. It loves water and grows in bogs or ponds. In Japan it is prized for its white and deep-violet flowers on graceful stems.

Iris ensata (formerly *Iris kaempferi* and so found in nearly all the literature), to give it its current name, is the most spectacular and popular of the Laevigatae series. These are the Japanese irises (known as Hanashobu in their homeland) developed by selective breeding of only one species over a period of three hundred years. The flowers of the wild species measure 3 to 4 inches but many of the cultivars of recent years can be as large as 8 to 10 inches with multiple petals and exotic patterns. These truly spectacular irises do not require such wet conditions as others in the Laevigatae series. They will grow beautifully in pots set in water or on pond edges but will also do well in a garden situation where they can receive abundant spring irrigation with regular but moderate irrigation thereafter.

SERIES HEXAGONAE – Louisiana irises

The species in the Hexagonae series also like wet conditions. The famous Louisiana irises overlap with the boundaries of *Iris virginica* and continue in the swamps and bays around the Gulf of Mexico coast and on to the state of Louisiana. Two species have headed north along the Mississippi River. The modern garden Louisiana irises are hybrids of these four species. *Iris giganticaerulea*, the largest species in both plant and flower, grows in the most southerly regions. *Iris fulva*, the smallest of the group with terracotta red flowers (a few yellows exist) is found from the coast of the Gulf of Mexico, on up the Mississippi as far north as Tennessee. *Iris nelsonii* (described by F. Randolph in 1966) is a hybrid population probably with a parentage of *Iris giganticaerulea* and *Iris fulva* that has gained specification in its local isolation in a swamp in Louisiana. This iris grows more like *Iris giganticaerulea*, but the flower resembles, in form and colour, a larger *Iris fulva*. The shorter *Iris brevicaulis* with lavender and blue flowers appearing on a zig-zag stem has been found growing as far north as Indiana but primarily comes from the south. Recent investigations have thrown doubt on the validity of a fifth species, *Iris hexagona*, which is the type for the series and grows along the southern Atlantic coast down into Florida.

The Louisiana irises are the greatest contribution from North America to the iris world. These southern cousins are not necessarily as beautiful or as spectacular as the Pacific Coast irises, but they are far more vigorous and adaptable to different garden situations. The Louisiana irises will grow and bloom in standing water or flourish in typical garden conditions if irrigation is good and the soil is acid.

Louisiana irises have a very wide range of colours, the widest to be found in the whole iris family, including the truest red in the iris world. These graceful and colourful irises make excellent flower arrangements.

SERIES CALIFORNICAE – Pacific Coast irises

The Pacific Coast irises, found on the west coast of North America, are among the most charismatic members of the genus. Their varied colours and patterns, and personality and charm, would have made them very popular, were it not for their lack of adaptability. They have only been grown successfully in their own restricted territory, which covers the states of Oregon, Washington and coastal California, or in locations with similar conditions, such as England and parts of New Zealand and Australia. This limited range is slowly being widened by selective breeding. Perhaps a less demanding strain will one day be developed.

The best way to experiment with these irises is to grow them from seed. Species in this series include *Iris douglasiana, Iris innominata*, and *Iris tenax*, among several others of lesser popularity and breeding potential.

SERIES SIBERICAE – Siberian irises

Series Sibericae is divided into two subseries according to chromosome counts: subseries Sibericae and Chrysographes. The subseries Sibericae with twenty-eight chromosomes is made up of only two species: *Iris sibirica* from eastern Europe and *Iris sanguinea* from north eastern Asia, while the subseries Chrysographes with forty chromosomes includes the blue-purple *Iris clarkei*, the yellow-flowered *Iris forrestii* and *Iris wilsonii*, the purple and violet *Iris chrysographes* and *Iris delavayi*, and some lesser known species. Subseries Chrysographes species have been crossed with the Californicae series to form the so-called Cal-Sibes, colourful but infertile hybrids. Fertile hybrids from crosses between the Sibericae and Chrysographes subseries have been produced, though less successfully. The forty-chromosome Siberians are not widely grown because of their need for extra moisture, acid soil and a particularly cold climate. The subseries Sibericae, on the other hand, grow in most gardens, though the best results are gained in moist, slightly acid conditions. Consequently, they are the most popular of the Siberian irises.

SUBSECTION EVANSIA – Crested irises

The Evansae series covers a wide-ranging group of irises and are a good example of species discontinuity between Asia and North America. Three species are found in the United States: *Iris tenuis*, from Oregon, *Iris lacustris* around the Great Lakes, and *Iris cristata* from Arkansas to the Atlantic. They have dainty, frilly blue-white flowers on tiny plants and grow in gravelly soil full of humus. They dislike arid areas, but otherwise are fairly easy to grow. A close relative, *Iris gracilipes*, is a wild flower in Japan and eastern Asia. These small irises have frilly lilac flowers on slightly taller stems, and could almost be mistaken for their Western relations. Though the Evansia group differ widely in form and habitat, the irises share the same cockscomb-like growth or crest which replaces the beard of the bearded irises.

The species with aerial rhizomes from the general area of southern China form the largest division of the group. These rhizomes do not grow under the ground but form what looks like a stout stem from the top of which the broad, yellow-green leaves fan out. The flat, very frilly flowers range in colour from white to pale lavender and measure only 2 to 3 inches according to species, with prominent, graphically traced patterns on the signal area of the falls. The many branches of the thin stems carry a multitude of flowers at all stages of bloom. These irises must be grown in the shade in hot and arid areas or in greenhouses in cold climates. As they seem to be allergic to soil, they have to be planted in coarse sand and decayed, or partially decayed, humus, such as wood shavings, leaves, or other such plant material.

In the wild the tallest of the species pushes its way through bushes to reach the light and so explains the need for the long rhizomes and the shade. The series is made up of the species *Iris confusa* (the tallest plant with the smallest flowers), *Iris wattii* (the most robust with the largest flower in light orchid) and *Iris japonica* (a self-sterile triploid form, which will cross with other species) that has gone wild in Japan, in spite of its Chinese origin.

The other species in this group, *Iris tectorum* – the 'roof iris' of Japan – is more commonly found in gardens, being easy to grow. The large flower protrudes from a short stem (10 to 15 inches) and a low-growing plant. The flower has many similarities with the shape of the bearded iris. Both have upright or rampant standards and flaring falls. Usually the flower is a mottled violet-lavender but there is also a white form. Indeed, *Iris tectorum* has been successfully crossed with the bearded *Iris pallida* several times, a fact which would indicate a closer relationship with the bearded irises rather than with the beardless. One such hybrid, 'Pal-Tec', makes an interesting and easy garden subject. Its name is derived from the two parents: *PAL-lida* and *TEC-torum*.

SERIES SPURIAE

All of the above-mentioned irises must be grown in acid soil. In fact, there are only a few beardless iris that require alkaline soil. Spuria irises not only prefer alkaline soils but they also need excellent drainage with a period of drying off for a couple of months in the summer. In their natural habitat they are flooded in the spring and baked dry in the summer. Apart from these requirements, the Spuria irises grow easily, and even abundantly, in temperate (Mediterranean) climates, though less well, but adequately, in colder areas. Most of the hybrids which have been named lie dormant in the summer and grow in the winter. A few varieties have summer-green foliage and are dormant in the winter. Both types require the same cultural procedures.

There are about fourteen species of Spuria irises ranging in height from 10-inch dwarfs to 4- or 5-feet-tall flowering stems. Most of these forty-chromosome cultivars originated by crossing the yellow-flowered *Iris monnieri* with the pollen of 'Monspur' then crossing the resulting seedlings with the white-flowered *Iris ochroleuca*. However, *Iris monnieri* has long been considered to be a hybrid and Dr Lee Lenz recently put forward the theory that it was a cross of *Iris ochroleuca* and *Iris xanthospuria*. Nor is 'Monspur' valid as a name any longer. The name is a combination of those that were considered to be its parents: *Iris MONnieri* and *Iris SPURia*. Recent chromosome counts, however, have established that *Iris spuria* could not be the parent.

Whatever the parentage is, this line introduced blue into the breeding lines. From these three colours — yellow, white and blue-lavender — all the many colours and shades of Spurias have been developed. The flowers range from wine red, mauve red, brown, bronze, beige pink, deep purple, violet, and blue to yellow, cream and white. A deep orange yellow was achieved by reintroducing *Iris xanthospuria* into the yellow line. The colour blue has been brought closer to the original shade by using *Iris carthaliniae* and *Iris klattii*. Hybrids from *Iris demetrii, Iris halophylla* and *Iris maritima* have been so prone to virus that they have been unusable for further work in breeding. Other Spuria varieties, however, have built up a resistance to this infection which can be passed on to their offspring. Breeders are making use of this ability in new work.

TETRAPLOIDY
No positive conclusions have been reached yet as to whether tetraploid forms of beardless irises have been found in the wild. Some breeders feel the forty-

chromosome Spuria irises reveal tetraploid characteristics. The wide range of colour is certainly unexpected in a diploid group. Another unusual feature of this series is the way the colours are expressed in the seedlings. A cross of the yellow cultivar 'Windfall' with the brown 'Driftwood' produced all of the colours in this group – yellow, brown, lavender, cream and white. Polyploidy has been discovered in two of the Hexagonae series in the wild – triploid forms of both *Iris giganticaerulea* ('Ruth Holleyman') and *Iris brevicaulis* ('Triple Treat'). If these could be crossed with the new induced tetraploids, great progress would be made.

Breeders have learnt to induce polyploidy artificially in most of the series except Spuriae. Tetraploid forms of Siberians, Japanese, and Louisianas are now available commercially and tetraploidy has been induced in *Iris laevigata, Iris pseudacorus, Iris tectorum* and others. Tetraploidy has not had the same effect on beardless irises as it did on tall bearded irises. The beardless tetraploid cultivars are slightly larger, with a little more colour than their diploid counterparts, but they have not, as yet, shown the impressive results of the bearded irises' development.

Societies and Awards

Throughout the world there are societies devoted to promoting interest in and knowledge of the iris. Many of them were founded as a result of the interest stimulated in iris breeding after the First World War. National iris societies may be found today in places as far afield as USA, Canada, England, France, Germany, Italy, Switzerland, South Africa, New Zealand, Australia and Japan. Membership of a society is the best way for the gardener to stay in touch with the developments and improvements of the genus. At present four national societies present annual awards to outstanding irises. These awards provide a useful guide for the gardener buying unknown irises.

The AMERICAN IRIS SOCIETY (AIS), founded in 1920, is the largest society. It has the important job of registering all new irises. It publishes books, including the invaluable *World of Irises* (1978), and quarterly bulletins full of useful information. Appointed judges of the AIS give annual awards to all classes of iris including Honorable Mention, Award of Merit and Dykes Medal, the most highly prized award which is presented by the British Iris Society. These awards are intended for all the iris sections. The following, however, exclude tall bearded irises: the Caparne-Welch Medal (for miniature dwarfs), the Cook-Douglas Medal (for standard dwarfs), the Sass Medal (for intermediate bearded), the Knowlton Medal (for border irises), the Williamson-White Award (for miniature tall bearded), the Ira Wood-Morgan Medal (for Siberian irises), the Mary Swords Debaillon Medal (for Louisiana irises), the Payne Award (for Japanese irises), the Eric Nies Award (for Spuria irises), and the Mitchell Award (for Californica irises).

BRITISH IRIS SOCIETY (BIS), founded in 1922, awards the annual Foster Memorial Plaque to an individual judged to have contributed the most to the advancement of the genus. It also judges and presents the Dykes Medal to the most outstanding iris of the year grown by a British hybridizer. This medal is also awarded through the AIS and the Iris Society of Australia. The BIS also presents Awards of Merit and Highly Commended Awards annually. It publishes periodic newsletters and the *Year Book*.

The IRIS SOCIETY OF AUSTRALIA judges the winner of the annual Dykes Medal, among others, though the award is presented by the BIS.

SOCIETÀ ITALIANA DELL'IRIS (The Italian Iris Society) presents the 'Premio Firenze' and several other awards in an annual international competition.

Commercialism

Considering that approximately 243 species of the iris have been listed by G. H. M. Lawrence in *Garden Irises* of 1959, incredibly few have become popular garden plants. There are only two of real commercial importance: the bulbous *Iris xiphium* with its two main types, the Dutch and the Spanish irises, which are largely used as cut flowers and *Iris pallida*, which is still grown in large numbers in Italy as a source of perfume. The aril iris species oncocyclus in its many forms, supplies a smaller market of cut flowers from Israel. The Spuria irises are beginning to get a corner of the cut-flower market, at least in California, due to the long time they can be preserved when refrigerated. However, the flowers do not last as long as the Dutch irises, but most of the buds will develop into flowers after the stalk is cut.

In commerical listings of garden irises a wide variety of beardless, and some of the bearded, irises such as dwarfs, medians, remontant and novelty irises can be found. But no iris in the entire genus even approaches the popularity of the tall bearded as a garden plant. You only have to see a field in full splendour to realize why the tall bearded iris holds a special place – second only to the rose – in the hearts of gardeners throughout the world.

'Kilt Lilt'

'Dusky Evening'

'Dusky Evening'

43

'Enchanted World'

'Navy Strut'

'Jeanne Price'

'Vivien'

'Spartan'

'Leda's Lover'

'Leda's Lover' ▷

'Country Lilac'

'Cosmic Dance'

'Constant Wattez"

'Prominent'

'Bettermint'

'Copper Mountain'

'Temple Gold'

'Silver Heather'

'Silver Heather' ▷

'Tampico'

'Gold Galore'

'Gentle Rain'

'Dusky Dancer'

65

'Pink Vanilla'

'Condottiere'

'Lovely Kay'

'Entourage'

'Entourage' ▷

'Victoria Falls'

'Schiaparelli'

'Lemon Mist'

'Rocket Red'

'Storm Center'

'Déjà Vu'

'Tropica'

'Virginia Squire'

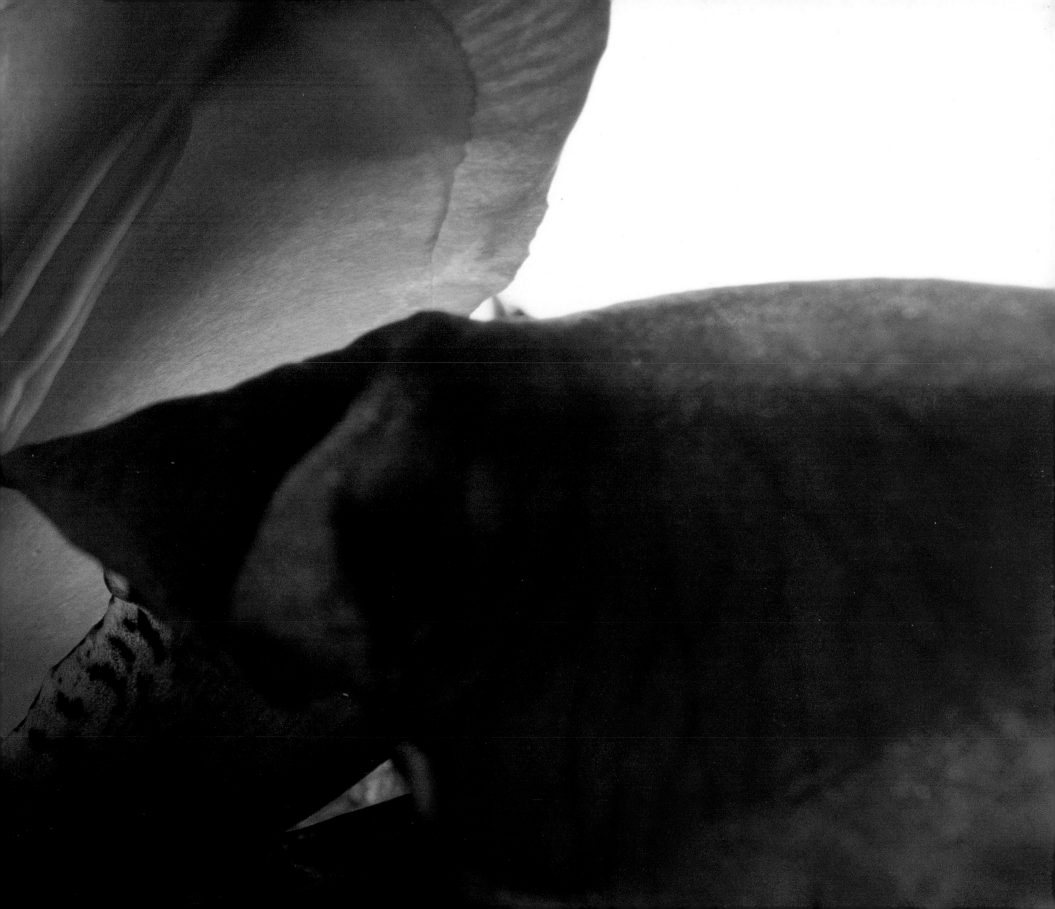

'Torch Parade'

'As de Coeur'

'Dazzling Gold'

'Mysterious'

'Embassadora'

'Valley West'

'Cardinal in Flight'

'Lacy Snowflake'

'Evening Echo'

'Silent Majesty'

'Betty Simon'

'Louise Watts'

'Velvet Flame'

'Lace Jabot'

'Dream Affair'

'Ghost Story'

'Ghost Story' ▷

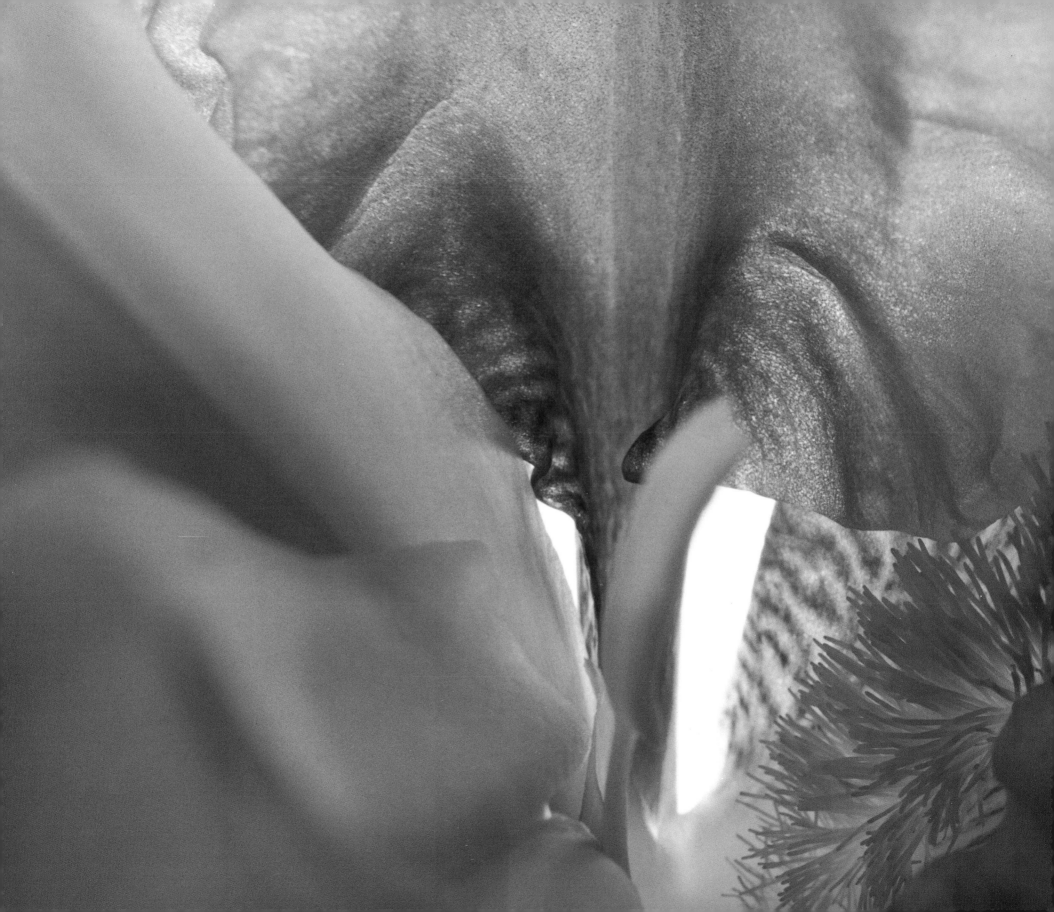

'Playgirl'

Incognita

'Mill Race'

'Fiction'

'Triumphant'

'Titan's Glory'

'Pink 'n' Mint'

'Jeanette'

'Jeanette' ▷

'Night Dragon'

'Lady Ilse'

'Quapaw'

'Love Chant'

115

'Pacific Mist'

'Raspberry Ripples'

'Java Dove'

'Chartreuse Ruffles

Notes on the Irises

'Kilt Lilt'

'Kilt Lilt'
Jim Gibson 1970
Dykes Medal 1976

'Dusky Evening'
Schreiner 1971

'Dusky Evening'
Schreiner 1971

'Enchanted World'
Schreiner 1979

PAGE 41   The bud of the iris flower is a beautiful but provocative mystery. What hidden delights are enclosed inside this tightly wrapped package? Turn to the final photograph and you will find out.

To an iris breeder, a bud at this stage of development presents an irresistible temptation, especially if it is the first of a seedling which has never bloomed before. Many iris growers and breeders have not been able to resist pulling apart the petals of the bud in order to see the beauty hidden within – and, of course, have done irreparable damage to the flower in the process. They can only wait for the next bud to open in its own time.

PAGE 42   This bud is at a very exciting stage of opening. The flower is clearly a bicolour, having standards (the petals that will remain upright) in one, usually lighter-toned, colour and the falls (the petals that will be down curving) in a contrasting, usually darker, shade. The contrast in colour is especially noticeable at this stage. The brownish-white standard is so unexpected from such a dark bud. The open flower is displayed in the next photograph.

PAGE 43   The bud in the previous photograph has now opened to reveal the full glory of the flower and the mature position of the standards and the falls. Another feature of the tall bearded iris is now apparent – the beards. All the flowers displayed in the book are variations on the theme of the tall *bearded* iris.

The beard has a definite purpose, as do most things in nature. It is designed to attract the pollinating insect to the parts of the flower in which it is most interested.

PAGE 44   The beards form the centre of the flower, the focal point of the overall design. They lead to the reproductive organs of the flower – and to its future. Breeders, attracted by the decorative potential of the beards, have experimented with the possible variations in colour. The original, and most common, shade is some variation of yellow, yet in this book the first seven photographs of irises with open petals all reveal beards of different colours. The lovely, ruffled, orchid pink, pictured on this page, for instance, has soft-orange beards, while the following photograph shows an iris with dark-blue beards.

'Navy Strut'
Schreiner 1974
Award of Merit 1975

'Jeanne Price'
Bennett Jones 1977

'Vivien'
K. Keppel 1979
Award of Merit 1984

'Spartan'
Schreiner 1973
Award of Merit 1976

PAGE 45   'Navy Strut' exhibits the nobility and the elegance inherent, and over the years enhanced, in this spectacular floral genus. The tall standards folded tightly at the top hide the splendour of the interior from view. The semi-flaring falls form an elegant downward arch. The charming fluting on all the petal edges lends the flower a less formal poise, while the deep-blue beards leading to the soul of the blossom add to the aura of mystery.

PAGE 46   Yellow – the colour so sought and so impressively achieved in the early tetraploid tall bearded irises and now given full and joyous expression through the camera's eye.

The branching of the stem is an important part of the display of the iris clump. Here we see the spur (a bud that is connected to the main stem) and the first branch (with the flower open). Below this should be at least two more branches with two or three buds at the end of each.

Off the top of the picture we would find the terminal cluster of buds, one of which is usually the first to open. Some stems will open three blossoms, from the terminal and two branches – the exhibitor's dream when choosing specimens for the annual iris show.

PAGE 47   This unusual angle is achieved by pulling the standards apart and looking directly down into the inner mysteries of the flower. It is an interesting view, and in the photograph, finely detailed. The prominent triumvirate of the style arms with the fin-like ridges leading up to and dividing the fancily serrated style crests and the brightly coloured contrasting beards pointing out from under the styles, all enshrined in the bowl of the standards – suggest a Byzantine tile design.

PAGE 48   Bearded irises do not possess the gene arrangement to produce a true red. There have been, however, many irises in reddish tones in the tetraploid tall bearded lines. *Iris variegata*, the diploid wild species, has varying amounts of reddish veining in the falls and is probably the original source of these shades in the later hybrids. Many of the reddish-toned tall bearded irises tend toward the brown side with a few toward the crimson. The glow of the afternoon sun behind some of the reddish flowers can produce a quite convincing impression of true red. The reddest tones in the bearded irises are in fact to be found in the standard dwarf flowers.

'Leda's Lover'
Ben R. Hager 1980
Award of Merit 1984

'Leda's Lover'
Ben R. Hager 1980
Award of Merit 1984

'Country Lilac'
Melba Hamblen 1971

'Cosmic Dance'
Schreiner 1982

PAGE 49　White on white. The impression of darker shades in the background is caused by the way the light has fallen. The soft glow of yellow in the heart of the flower gives an effect of staged lighting.

If the god Zeus in the ancient myth had this much charisma in his swan costume, perhaps Leda's resistance to his advances was an exaggeration.

PAGES 50 AND 51　When the camera lens peers into the interior of the flower, we can see the cause of the golden glow in the heart of the flower. The yellow centre is undoubtedly why this iris is usually described as a 'warm white' as opposed to a 'cool white' which has a blue influence. Photographing a white iris against a white background requires great skill to achieve the correct balance of light and shade.

PAGE 52　The usual colour arrangement in bicoloured irises consists of lighter-toned standards and darker falls. An interesting reversal of the norm is seen in the iris pictured here which features medium-toned, lavender-purple standards and white falls with lavender tints. This pattern is known as reverse bicolour. Bright tangerine beards will brighten up nearly any colour combination.

PAGE 53　The dark colouring of the petals with paler areas of illumination on the falls may be a reminder of the galaxy with its vast areas of darkness and pinpoints of light.

The names of irises are often as intriguing as the flowers themselves. A good name can be worth a thousand words, capturing the poetic beauty of the flower itself.

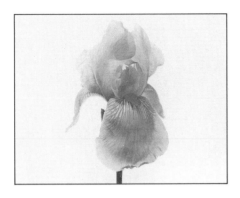

'Constant Wattez'
Piet van Veen 1959

'Prominent'
Glen Corlew 1980

'Bettermint'
Joe Ghio 1979

'Copper Mountain'
Schreiner 1978

PAGE 54 'Constant Wattez' is an example of the next generation of flowers to appear after the pink revolution. One parent of this flower was the pink iris 'Edward Windsor' (registered as such but often called 'Edward of Windsor'). Neither parent of 'Edward Windsor' nor any iris in the preceding lineage was pink; the colour first appeared in 'Edward Windsor'. The form of 'Constant Wattez' is 'old-fashioned', the strong veining on the upper part of the falls no longer being considered *de rigueur*. Forty years ago, however, it made quite an impression. When the iris in this photograph is compared with those on pages 68 and 102, the progress made by iris breeders in flower form, colour and overall appeal can be appreciated.

PAGE 55 Smoothness of colour saturation is much admired in the iris flower. Equal distribution of the pigment allows the full impact of the colour to be admired. In this photograph the tangerine beards are subdued. They add a bit of contrast but do not overpower the smooth lavender colour of the petals. The real contrast is historical: the depth and consistency of the lavender colouring as exhibited in a modern iris is a far cry from the watery transparency of the varieties developed in the early years of iris breeding.

PAGE 56 Where we see a greenish cast in the colouring of iris petals, the camera often does not, rather interpreting the shading as tan or light brown. Which is correct, the camera or the eye? The beauty of the flower is not impaired just because we cannot give a label to the colour.

PAGE 57 Few flowers in nature are brown. Of those that are brown, fewer still have the beautiful, rich and attractive colours found in irises. There are many shades – copper brown, red brown, leather brown, buff brown. These are the colours of the desert landscapes in which some irises are found. Choosing a suitable name for a new iris flower can have its problems, considering that the names already in use run to six volumes and cannot be repeated. Finding a name that describes the flower and at the same time has a pleasant and memorable sound is often as difficult as producing a 'new' iris in the first place.

'Temple Gold'
Walt Luihn 1978

'Silver Heather'
David Niswonger 1978

'Silver Heather'
David Niswonger 1978

'Tampico'
Walt Luihn 1978

PAGE 58   Does this photograph suggest oriental architecture overlaid with gold leaf? The Golden Pavilion in Japan comes to mind. The exterior of the flower could also suggest a pagoda effect. The only thing lacking is surrounding water to reflect back the temple in all its shining glory.

PAGE 59   The name gives an accurate picture of the colour of this iris: silvery lavender, smooth and pastel – a portrait of sheer elegance. It was probably those tangerine beards that really caught your attention, or will do in the following photograph.

PAGES 60 AND 61   The eyecatching beards dominate the photograph, surrounded as they are by the misty, silvery lavender tones. The veining in the standards is also more prominent than in the previous photograph. The upward sweep of the veins gives an indication of the upper reaches of the standards which are out of sight.

PAGE 62   A true red may not appear in iris flowers, but these rich, ruby-brown tones are nevertheless very striking.

'Gold Galore'
Schreiner 1978
Award of Merit 1982

'Gentle Rain'
Keith Keppel 1977
Award of Merit 1980

'Dusky Dancer'
Walt Luihn 1967
Award of Merit 1970

'Pink Vanilla'
Larry Gaulter 1979

PAGE 63 More irises have been developed and marketed under the Schreiner family name than any other. Awards have followed in equal share. The Schreiner family has been in the business of distributing irises since 1924 and goes back three generations.

'Gold Galore' is one of the most popular of the Schreiner irises though it has not won a Dykes Medal as five other Schreiner irises have.

PAGE 64 Keith Keppel shares the throne with Jim Gibson ('Kilt Lilt', on pages 41 and 120) in the kingdom of the plicatas. The plicata pattern is so varied and intricate that two breeders can work in this field and still turn out noticeably different irises.

This photograph features a plicata bicolour: the dark standards contrast with the white falls which are marked with both types of plicata design – peppering and stitching.

PAGE 65 Among the most intriguing colours in irises are the so-called 'blacks'. The colour is not a true black but it is close enough to make little difference. This iris surely has some of the blackest tones of any competing flower with the possible exception of eremus. If the flower is lit from behind, rays of purple will appear as the light penetrates the petals. Shine the light from the front and the flower shows very little colour.

PAGE 66 This is a view through the Byzantium-like arch into the domed gallery of the temple dedicated to the earth goddess of fertility. It is light and warm inside.

Larry Gaulter's work almost spans the whole history of modern iris breeding. In his youth he was associated with the early 'greats' such as the Sass brothers and others. He is still in the picture today, introducing irises through Cooley's Iris Gardens in Oregon.

'Condottiere'
Jean Cayeux 1978

'Lovely Kay'
Melba Hamblen 1980
Award of Merit 1984

'Entourage'
Joe Ghio 1977
Award of Merit 1980

'Entourage'
Joe Ghio 1977
Award of Merit 1980

PAGE 67   Jean Cayeux, commercial grower of irises in Gien, France, and prolific hybridizer, belongs to the famous French family whose immediate ancestors were Ferdinand and René Cayeux, originators of many of the important early tetraploids, such as 'Vert Galant', 'Député Nomblot', 'Jean Cayeux' and many others. Jean Cayeux is currently carrying on the family tradition.

The emphasis in this photograph is laid on the beard, which stands as a beacon at the top of the wide, blue-violet landing pad with the whole blue sky towering above.

There are those who prefer the tailored-look for an iris flower, but who could deny the grace and beauty of these provocative waved and fluted petals?

PAGE 68   Kay Nelson has been the registrar for the international iris registry (compiled and published under the auspices of the American Iris Society) for over twenty years. She is indeed a *lovely* person both spiritually and physically.

The consistent quality of the pink colouring and the toned-down tangerine beards form the goals of breeders who are working towards improving pink irises. Progress happens in a cumulative way, with the improvements made in one generation being passed on to the next. For this reason, knowledge of the parentage of an iris is essential for iris breeders.

PAGE 69   The outside . . .

PAGES 70 AND 71 . . . and the inside.

'Victoria Falls'
Schreiner 1977
Dykes Medal 1984

'Schiaparelli'
Steve Moldovan 1971

'Lemon Mist'
Nathan Rudolph 1972
Award of Merit 1975

'Rocket Red'
Schreiner 1984

PAGE 72   This photograph surely reveals the aptness of the name of this iris. Blue water cascades from above, producing the foam of the white beard as it goes over the edge of the precipice. The combination of the flower, the breeder who named it, and the photographer creates a charming success.

PAGE 73   Pink irises generally share certain common features. On the whole they display soft, ethereal qualities fitting for their delicate tones. All have tangerine beards, as shown in this photograph.

PAGE 74   The name is particularly apt for this iris, perfectly describing its clear, crisp and yellow tones. The fresh colour of the standards contrasts with the frosty-white areas in the falls, the whole being set off by the orange beards. Seen in a group in the garden, these irises make an attractive and invigorating show.

PAGE 75   The darker-toned irises make a valuable contribution to the arrangement of any garden. They provide an interesting focal point when planted among irises of paler, pastel shades. But those with a critical eye should be warned: this reddish-maroon colouring will not blend well with pinks or blues. Dark violets are better with the latter groups and dark browns give an extra glow to pinks and yellows. These observations are made from a human viewpoint, though Mother Nature has no qualms about matching colours when sowing a field of wild flowers.

'Storm Center'
Schreiner 1979

'Déjà Vu'
Bryce Williamson 1974

'Tropica'
Joe Ghio 1983

'Virginia Squire'
Larry Gaulter 1973

PAGE 76   Even in nature things do not always work to plan. At some time in the development of this flower confusion arose over the form – two falls emerged where there should only be one. The two grew together and created an extra wide fall with two beards, side by side, instead of one. Nature does not often make mistakes, though it did in this case.

PAGE 77   The ghostly feeling that we have already experienced something which is in fact occurring for the first time is best translated to colour in the grey and atmospheric tones of lavender or mauve, as displayed in this photograph. So let us present this iris with the award for the most appropriate name.

Another striking feature of this iris can be seen in the way the smooth brown mauve of the standards seeps through the golden tan of the hafts to the lavender of the full fall petals. The blue at the tips of the orange beards adds the final touch to a true symphony of harmonious colour.

PAGE 78   This iris has been given the brand name of a frozen Florida orange juice. The choice is most appropriate; never before has an iris flower come so close to the colour of pure, unadulterated orange juice. The full effect of the deep colour can only really be appreciated in the garden setting.

PAGE 79   This view from the underside of the flower reveals the supports flaring out from the spathes at the ends of the stem and holding the outstretched falls in a grand panoply. Sometimes it is rewarding to peek into places not intended for general viewing.

'Virginia Squire'
Larry Gaulter 1973

'Torch Parade'
William Bledsoe 1979

'As de Coeur'
Jean Cayeux 1978

'Dazzling Gold'
D. C. Anderson 1981
Award of Merit 1985

PAGES 80 AND 81   Are we sitting by a camp fire surrounded by an impressionistic forest? Or are there heavy draperies threatening to envelop us in dark dreams? Virginia, where are you?

PAGE 82   If several rhizomes of an iris such as this are planted in a row, the tall stems carrying these tangerine-to-apricot flowers with their saturn-red beards will bloom to resemble a parade of torches ablaze in the spring sunlight.

The apricot, orange, salmon, peach and pink colours are all variations of the 'pink revolution' described earlier. All pink irises will carry the so-called tangerine beards.

PAGE 83   The fantastic tangerine-bearded white irises are another gift of the 'pink revolution'. Although the whites share the same general genetic make-up as the tangerine-bearded pink irises, the genes that cause the pink colouring have mutated. Either genes that produce a white which will not allow the pink colour to appear (the *dominant white* condition) have resulted or the genes that encourage pink colour have just disappeared (the *recessive* condition). In spite of the lack of pink colouring, the tangerine-flame beards stand out predominantly against the white background.

If two recessive tangerine whites are crossed, the offspring will all be tangerine whites. If recessive and dominant tangerine whites or two dominant tangerine whites are crossed, the offspring will be coloured white, pink or orchid and have tangerine beards.

PAGE 84   For vivid colouring this short iris has no match. Its full orange yellow grabs your attention immediately and compensates for any deficiency in height. The bright brown-red veining does nothing to lessen the dazzling impression in any way. Rather it accentuates the effect. The pattern ranges in different flowers from almost solid reddish overlay to sketchily dotted petals.

'Mysterious'
Schreiner 1974

'Embassadora'
Barry Blyth 1978–79

'Valley West'
Melba Hamblen 1973

'Cardinal in Flight'
William Schortman 1979

PAGE 85   In order to photograph this unobstructed view of the reproductive system of the iris flower, the fall must be pulled down. The shape of the flower is distorted considerably, though in the name of science it is acceptable.

The style arm is clearly presented. The pollen on the two parted anthers clings to the inner arch of the style arm. Near the end of the arm lies the stigmatic lip to which the pollen must be moved for fertilization to take place. The decorative petaloid style crests protect the lip from above. We can also see that the beards do lead all the way down to the bottom of the petals where the nectar can be found by the bumble bees.

PAGE 86   A small hybrid iris named 'Progenitor' has been mentioned earlier. It was an ugly little standard dwarf, but it carried a gene that inhibited the colour in the standards of most iris flowers to which it was related. 'Embassadora', depicted in this photograph, is the result of crossing a self-coloured iris (one with both standards and falls the same colour) with one of the hundreds of existing progeny of 'Progenitor'. In all cases the resulting seedlings have white, cream, pale-blue, or yellow standards and deeper-coloured falls. 'Embassadora' must come from a long line of tangerine-bearded pink ancestors; even though the pink colouring is suppressed, the flower has inherited the bright tangerine beards. It originated in Australia.

PAGE 87   Only a very wide-petalled iris flower could be the representative of the vast valleys and majestic mountains of the western states of the USA where this iris was born and bred.

The part of the flower brought to our attention in this photograph is the intricate veining, nearly always in a deeper colour. These 'blood vessels' of the flower carry the nutrients and moisture throughout the petals and so keep the beauty of form and colour for the whole three days of the flower's life. When these veins cease to function, the flower withers and dies, but is usually replaced by another flower through which the nutrients and moisture are rerouted.

PAGE 88   A memory, a flicker of red glimpsed through the shadowy dense woods; and then a flash of brighter red as a sly sunbeam penetrates the leaves of the trees before disappearing again into the shadows.

It would have to be a memory as there are no cardinals in California where this flower first bloomed. But it is comforting to have memories, especially when they take such a lovely form as this friendly, deep-red iris.

'Lacy Snowflake'
Schreiner 1977
Award of Merit 1982

'Lacy Snowflake'
Schreiner 1977
Award of Merit 1982

'Evening Echo'
Melba Hamblen 1977

'Silent Majesty'
Melba Hamblen 1977
Award of Merit 1981

PAGE 89   Most photographers concentrate on the whiteness of the petals and the frilly, lacy petal edges when capturing this flower. Our photographer, however, ignores these attributes. Instead he has looked for colour in what is usually considered an all-white flower. He seeks yellow-gold veining in the throat and the white beards sprinkled with bright yellow.

PAGES 90 AND 91   One photograph is not enough to give a convincing impression of the rich colour in the golden heart of this flower and so our photographer digs deeper. At the centre yellow merges to near brown — but a cooling white mist is found there as well.

This handsome portrait clearly shows the pollen-carrying anther with the wavy line of the stigmatic lip above.

PAGE 92   The colours of beards hold a fascination for both breeders and lovers of irises. Such is the interest that a whole range of beard colours have been cultivated and can now be found in gardens everywhere. In nature the colours are more stable. The variety has arisen from man's compulsion to seek out the new and different wherever possible. Perhaps the dramatic example of beard colouring displayed in this photograph will help us to understand this driving force.

PAGE 93   This flower possesses one of the most effective colours that the iris family can produce: deep, glowing violet, consistent (even in the beards) and commanding in a garden setting. Few other flowering plants can create such a silky texture or satisfying saturation of colour.

'Betty Simon'
Melba Hamblen 1976
Award of Merit 1979

'Louise Watts'
Clarence Blocher 1971
Award of Merit 1976

'Velvet Flame'
Joe Gatty 1978

'Lace Jabot'
Larry Gaulter 1982

PAGE 94   Pastel colour tones are prominent in flowers growing in natural environments because lighter shades of colour reflect more light and so are visible at greater distances. Attraction is the name of the game. The more pollinating insects are lured towards the iris, the more progeny is produced.

The human eye is drawn to this iris not so much by its ability to reflect light but by its numerous other qualities: harmony and smoothness of colour, density of tone, sparkle, and texture.

PAGE 95   The iris breeder watches for and attempts to capture various nuances in new cultivars such as eye-catching variations in colour shading, patterns, intensities and light reflection. The flower in this photograph would attract attention because of the different emphasis in colour which it brings to the garden. Most bicolour forms will depend on deeper colouration in the falls and more airy, pale tones in the upward-reaching standards. An iris with the reverse colouring such as 'Louise Watts' with its berry-mauve standards and lightly tinted, but oyster-white, falls makes its mark by its charismatic individuality.

PAGE 96   This intimate, close-up and magnified view clearly illustrates the structure of the petals as they rise from the triad base in an almost geodesic pattern of veining. The light shining through the translucent petals creates an effect of gleaming coloured glass, and bathes the upreaching style arms, poised like dancers' hands, in a rich berry glow.

PAGE 97   'Lace Jabot' contains many of the features which are admired by iris growers today. Among these are width of petal, standards that touch or overlap over the top of the flower, decorative ruching and ruffling of the petal edges, and clean, smooth application of colour with as little vein patterning as possible in the throat of the flower. Iris *aficionados* also look for a vigorous plant with well-branched stems and numerous buds under the flower.

'Dream Affair'
Joe Gatty 1987

'Ghost Story'
Joe Ghio 1975

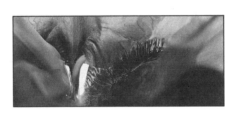

'Ghost Story'
Joe Ghio 1975

'Playgirl'
Joe Gatty 1977
Award of Merit 1980

PAGE 98   A tightly folded bud awaits beneath the spread of the gold and cream panoply of the open flower, dreaming of its turn to display its beauty to the world. If you could see through the green spathe below, you would find yet another undeveloped bud dreaming of its future glory.

PAGE 99   The ghostly substance, ectoplasm, is usually depicted as a grey-white, formless mist, floating just above the ground. The colour of 'Ghost Story' in this photograph seems right, but just for curiosity let's look . . .

PAGES 100 AND 101   . . . inside. Ah, here is the haunting, misty ectoplasm floating through eerie corridors of evil décor, fungal growths and mystical movements of light-play . . .

PAGE 102   'Playgirl' – a voluptuously provocative iris. Flowers in this soft-pink colour with ruffled petals are capable of creating a romantic dream or fantasy, especially when the heart of the flower is aglow with the light from flame-coloured beards.

Incognita

'Mill Race'
Larry Gaulter 1975

'Fiction'
Bryce Williamson 1978

'Triumphant'
Glen Corlew 1980

PAGE 103   It is almost impossible to find an iris garden in which every flower is labelled with the correct cultivar name. There is always at least one that is kept in the garden for various reasons – for its shade of colour, intriguing pattern, vigorous growth and display or for sentimental memories – even though the name has been lost.

PAGE 104   Blue is a popular colour in flowers, although it occurs rarely among most common garden plants. It does arise, in 'Plumbago', 'Bachelor Buttons' and 'Ceanothus' (Californian mountain lilac), though violet and purple shades appear more frequently. Irises are particularly noted for their many variations on effective, though not always true, blue, with a range from palest blue white all the way to deep sea blue.

PAGE 105   The usually flamboyant plicata patterns (coloured stitching and peppering aroud the edge of the basically lighter tone of the petal) can be found in pastel shades as well. These irises take on a completely different personality from other varieties in the iris garden. The flower in this photograph looks as though a mist of purple has spread over the white ground and has seeped beneath the creamy cloud of the fluted standards.

PAGE 106   Blue banners, wind whipped and carried aloft above the ranks of the passing parade, stand upright with the bold insignia of the bright beards blowing about in the wind.

There is something about the iris that inspires the invention of metaphors for the purpose of description.

'Titan's Glory'
Schreiner 1981
Dykes Medal 1988

'Pink 'n' Mint'
Schreiner 1979

'Jeanette'
Mark Rogers 1977

'Jeanette'
Mark Rogers 1977

PAGE 107   Not without reason is this iris one of the current favourites of the iris world. The deep royal colour so beautifully captured in the photograph can best be appreciated as a living example during the spring in the garden.

PAGE 108   The green colour of the leaves and stems is correctly captured by the camera. The green tint does indeed exist in the flowers of some varieties, though the camera sometimes fails to catch it. In this photograph a hint of green is visible on the falls near the beards. In fact, this is about as much green as will occur in the living specimen of this variety.

PAGE 109   In this classical view of the iris flower, as nature intended us to see it, a clear definition of floral parts is shown. Of course innumerable variations are possible, leading to an unending source of joy and pleasure.

PAGES 110 AND 111   Another view of the iris on the previous page directs our attention to specific details: the unique beards leading into the very heart of the flower, the decorative veining on the fall hafts (sometimes acceptable but at most times frowned on by the connoisseur), and the very precise yellow borders surrounding the pristine white falls. This photograph presents the details of the flower as opposed to the classical presentation of the previous one.

'Night Dragon'
Franklin Carr 1978

'Lady Ilse'
Kenneth Smith 1951
Award of Merit 1955

'Quapaw'
Richard Butler 1976

'Love Chant'
Barry Blyth 1979–80

PAGE 112   Could this be a dragon crouching in his dark lair and gazing out into the brilliantly lit world through the entrance to his cave? It is, of course, another photograph taken again from an unusual angle. We are thus privileged to see the patterns and colours which are normally obscured from view.

PAGE 113   Pretty, cool, blue irises give such satisfaction. Surely no other flower can soothe the spirit or calm the nerves in the same way as a collection of blue irises in full bloom, gently swaying in the breeze and sparkling in the spring sunshine.

PAGE 114   The American Indian is no longer a vanishing race, but spiritually most native Americans are still disorientated, even though they are living on land occupied by their ancestors for centuries past. Perhaps naming an iris after one of the tribes acts as a small tribute and some sort of recognition.

PAGE 115   Perhaps 'the fairies at the bottom of the garden' could use such a flower as a pink parasol, though the falls are not large enough to provide adequate covering. The photograph is taken from an unusual angle, highly appropriate for this iris from 'down under' (Australia).

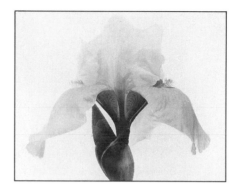

'Pacific Mist'
Schreiner 1979
Award of Merit 1984

'Raspberry Ripples'
David Niswonger 1969
Award of Merit 1972

'Java Dove'
Gordon Plough 1964
Award of Merit 1967

'Chartreuse Ruffles'
Nathan Rudolph 1976
Award of Merit 1979

PAGE 116   Blue mist swirling above the breaking blue waves – that could be the impression created by the photograph, even though, putting imagination on one side, we know we are looking at the intricate architecture of the flower centre.

To the layman this photograph could be an 'Art Nouveau' representation: a field of colour offered as an imaginative art form to stimulate personal interpretations.

PAGE 117   The fruity colours in some iris flowers seem intended to whet our appetites rather than to attract bees. In this way nature may have conceived another ingenious method of distribution. In the original plan, insects would be attracted to the flower and would start the process of pollination, leading to seed setting and distribution and thus to a new generation. The process would be repeated over and over again. Yet the aesthetic appeal may have done more to transport the iris to the far corners of the globe than any other.

PAGE 118   The popular amoena pattern is defined as 'pure white standards and coloured falls'. The most difficult combination of colour to achieve in this pattern has been the 'pink amoena' (white standards and pink falls). 'Java Dove' with its pinkish falls is the result of early experimentation, though there has been no great improvement on the colours of this iris in the current market. It is one of the challenges left for breeders of new irises.

PAGE 119   As the name implies, this iris is usually a mixture of green and yellow colouring. The camera in this particular case has concentrated on the yellow tones of the flower. Out of sight is the lacy border around the edges of the petals, which is primarily responsible for the name. The photograph does show the attractive style crests whose borders are filled with lace.

'Kilt Lilt'
Jim Gibson 1970
Dykes Medal 1976

PAGE 120   The bud featured on page
41 has now opened, flaunted its beauty
for three days and disappeared.
Fortunately another bud has developed
and is showing off its full bloom for your
pleasure – and a third bud is yet to open.

This dramatic flower is an example of
the fancy plicata pattern, with laced petal
edges. The shining bronze standards are
only lightly speckled, but the white
ground falls are almost completely
covered with a dark-brown pattern. This
photograph provides the best illustration
of the term 'lace'. The petal edges of the
falls are intricately crinkled and gathered
into a formation that resembles decorative
lace borders. This feature has become
quite popular in recent years.

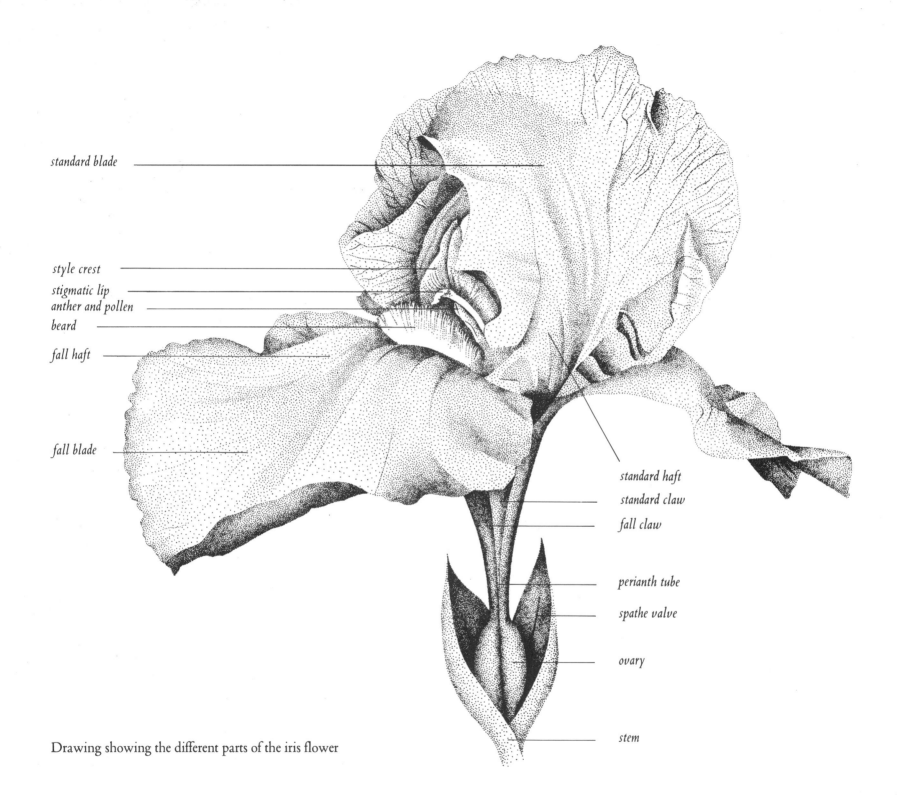

standard blade

style crest

stigmatic lip

anther and pollen

beard

fall haft

fall blade

standard haft

standard claw

fall claw

perianth tube

spathe valve

ovary

stem

Drawing showing the different parts of the iris flower

Bibliography

Dykes, W. R., *The Genus Iris* (1913)

Dykes, W. R., *A Handbook of Garden Irises* (1924)

Dykes, W. R., *Irises* (1930)

DuBose, Sidney P., *Personal Correspondence* (1988)

Hoegler, Rudolf G., and Oliver Reverdin, *Crete in Colour* (1961)

Lawrence, G. H. M., *Garden Irises* (1959)

Lenz, Dr Lee, 'The chromosomes of the Spuria irises and the evolution of the garden forms', *Aliso* (1963)

Matt, Leonard von, and Stylianos Alexiou, Nikolaos Platon, Hanni Guanelli, *Ancient Crete*
(translated by D. J. S. Thomson 1968)

Mitchell, Sydney B., *Iris for Every Garden* (1949)

Simonet, Marc, *The Genus Iris: Cytological and Genetic Research* (translated by Bee Warburton 1980)

Warburton, Bee, and Melba Hamblen (eds.), *The World of Irises* (1978)